# Four Seasons of
# QUILLING™

# Table of Contents

| | | | |
|---|---|---|---|
| **2** | Quilling Basics | **14** | Summer Tree |
| **3** | Quilled Shape Gallery | **17** | Autumn Tree |
| **6** | Four Seasons Tree Sampler | **19** | Winter Tree |
| **12** | Spring Tree | **24** | Buyer's Guide |

# Quilling Basics

### Getting Started

To launch your adventure in quilling, all you'll need are a few basic tools and supplies. Your first purchase should be either a slotted or needle quilling tool. For beginners, a slotted tool is helpful in holding the ends of quilling strips securely as you start to roll paper strips. As you advance your skills, a needle tool will allow you to create smaller, more professional-looking centers in your quilled shapes. Both tools are available at craft stores and online.

You'll also want to purchase quilling strips. These are available in single- or multicolored packs as well as various widths. For practice, use a paper trimmer and text-weight paper to cut your own quilling strips.

### Quilling With a Slotted Tool

To use the slotted tool, slide the end of a paper quilling strip into the slot. Turn the tool as directed with one hand as you guide the paper strip with the other to create a basic paper coil.

Apply a tiny amount of glue to the end of the coil and hold it in place for a few moments to dry. The finished coil can be used as is or pinched into any desired shape. To create additional quilled shapes, refer to the Quilled Shape Gallery on pages 3–5. Alternatively, you may leave the coil end unglued and use the rolled strip as a loose scroll or form it into a shaped scroll.

### Quilling With a Needle Tool

If you prefer a coil not to have the center crimp that a slotted tool produces, create your shapes with a needle tool. Quilling with a needle tool requires some practice to achieve an evenly rolled coil with a tiny, round center.

Using the thumb and index finger of whichever hand feels most comfortable for you, roll the paper around the needle using relaxed, even pressure, while holding the handle steady with the other hand.

### Gluing Your Quilling

Many different glues are available to crafters, and each person seems to have a favorite when it comes to quilling. The main thing is to use only a scant amount as no glue should show on a finished project.

The most commonly recommended glue is any brand that dries clear. The main thing to remember is to use a very small amount so that no glue shows on your finished piece.

To apply glue to coils, many quillers use a refillable, precision-tip glue bottle. You can also dip the point of a paper piercer, T-pin or toothpick into a puddle of glue, then carefully apply to your quilled shape.

It is helpful to work on a nonstick craft sheet or waxed paper while assembling quilled components with glue.

When gluing assembled quilling to cardstock or mat board, spread a thin layer of craft glue on a nonstick surface. Hold the quilled shape with tweezers, touch the underside to glue and place directly on the backing surface. Avoid sliding the quilling into position as this will leave a shiny trail of glue. ■

**Designer's T!P**

*When making cards, use double-sided adhesive to secure cardstock or paper layers to a card front. A glue stick can also be used and allows for a bit of repositioning, but the layers may not hold as well long-term.*

# Quilled Shape Gallery

By Shelly Krzyzewski & Ann Martin

## Scrolls

### C Scroll
Roll each end of strip toward center; the midsection will curve gracefully.

### V Scroll
Fold strip in half and roll each end outward.

### Modified V Scroll
Fold strip in half. Roll one end away from fold and the other end toward fold.

### Y Scroll
Fold the strip of paper in half and roll the ends outward like a V Scroll. Spread glue between the strips at the base and press together.

### Heart Scroll
Fold strip in half and roll each end inward toward midpoint.

## Coils

### Tight Coil
Roll strip on tool and adhere end in place without allowing coil to relax. Slide coil off tool.

### Domed Tight Coil (Grape Roll)
Form a Tight Coil and gently push up from underside of coil with the ball of a glass-head pin or fingers. Apply a thin coat of glue inside dome to hold rounded shape.

### Loose (Closed) Coil
Roll one end of strip and slide coil off tool. Tighten coil or allow it to relax to create coil of desired size; adhere end to outer edge.

### Ring Coil
Use a cylindrical object to form a ring of desired size. Wrap strip around the object several times; adhere end and slide coil off object.

### Teardrop
Form a Loose (Closed) Coil. Pinch the joining spot to create a point.

### Marquise
Form a Loose (Closed) Coil. Pinch opposite sides to create two points, taking care to keep coil center positioned in center of Marquise.

### Shaped Marquise
Form a Marquise. Grasp pointed ends; curve one end upward and the other end downward.

### Crescent
Form a Teardrop. Pinch a second point not directly opposite the first, and bend points toward each other.

## Additional Shape

### Spiral

Continuously wrap paper strip around a needle tool or thin, stiff wire without overlapping edges. While strip is still on tool, hold each end of spiral and twist gently to tighten. Slide straight off tool.

## Flowers

### Basic Fringed Flower

A Fringed Flower can be made with a strip of almost any width and length. A standard-size strip would be ⅜ x 3 inches. Use detail scissors to make fine side-by-side cuts across width of strip. Snip as far into the strip as possible without cutting all the way through. If you accidentally cut through the strip, adhere the ends together at the break and continue.

Roll fringed strip in the same manner as a Tight Coil. Adhere end, remove from tool and fluff fringe open. To give the flower a natural look, use blade of scissors to curve fringe downward, as if curling paper ribbon.

### Folded Rose

A Folded Rose can be made with a strip of almost any width and length. A standard-size strip would measure ⅜ x 7 inches. Narrower strips, such as ¼ inch or even ⅛ inch, would result in a smaller rose or bud.

Slip end of strip into slotted tool from the left. Holding the tool vertically in right hand and the strip in left hand, roll the tool clockwise to the left a few times to secure the paper. This will be the center of the rose.

With left hand, fold the paper strip up at a 90-degree angle. Continue to roll the tool toward the left, rolling over the fold. At the same time, gently lower the strip with left hand to return it to a horizontal position.

Repeat this folding-and-rolling process until you reach the end of the strip. Slip rose (which has formed upside down) off the tool, allow it to relax, and shape folds gently as desired. Snip off excess strip length and hide end by gluing it under rose.

### Pompom Flower

Fringe the full length of two ⅜-inch strips in complementary colors.

Once fringed, tear both strips to 8 inches. **Note:** *Retain remaining length of fringed pieces to create additional flowers. Adjust length and width of strips to change size of flowers.*

Adhere one fringed strip on top of the other.

Using a slotted quilling tool, roll entire length of strip, placing a dab of quick-drying adhesive at every second or third turn. Adhere end; let dry.

Fluff the flower open to create a pompom.

## Husking Basics

*Note: Use these steps as indicated in the instructions for the husked pieces in the Summer and Autumn tree sections.*

**1.** Copy the husking pattern on ¼-inch graph paper; place the graph over cork tile.

**2.** Wrap the end of a strip of quilling paper around one pin and glue it as an anchor point. Insert the pin at the first numbered dot. Wrap the paper around a pin in each dot in number order, returning to the bottom of the first pin point.

**3.** Once all pins have been placed and paper looped around them, use the remaining paper to wrap around the perimeter of the husked shape, gluing at the point of every loop.

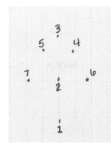

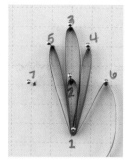

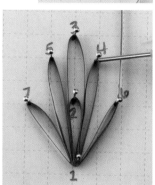

## Tuck & Roll Joining Technique

Use multiple lengths of quilling paper to create a larger Tight Coil (or other shape) by wrapping one length of quilling paper with slotted quilling tool. Stop wrapping 4–5 inches from end. Tuck a new length of quilling paper under partially wrapped end of quilling paper, making sure paper grain is going in the same direction. Continue wrapping shape. Repeat until desired size of quilled shape has been created. Adhere end of last quilling paper length wrapped. ■

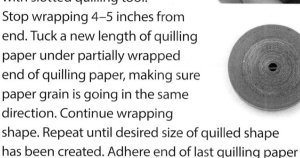

# Four Seasons Tree Sampler

## Materials

Cardstock: white, light green, medium green, moss green

Text-weight paper: pink, light pink, dark pink, blue, light blue, lavender

1/16-inch-wide quilling paper strips: red, pink, blue, orange, white

1/8-inch-wide quilling paper strips: yellow, purple, violet, lavender, cadet blue, orange, bright yellow, fuchsia, pink, light pink, holiday green, moss green, red, brown, deep red, melon, silver/gray, light brown, various shades of brown

3/8-inch-wide quilling paper strips: brown, lavender, bright yellow, deep rose, orange, magenta, white, bright yellow, melon, turquoise

5/8-inch-wide quilling paper strips: brown, deep rose, lavender, bright yellow

Quilling tools: needle (or hatpin or toothpicks), slotted

Punches: EK Success (3-Lobe Leaf, Martha Stewart Medium Monarch Butterfly); McGill (1-inch Stacking Daisies)

Quilling circle template

Self-closing tweezers

Mat board or other backing for tree

Cork tile

1/4-inch graph paper

Sticky notes

Embossing stylus

Straight pins

Ruler

Small scissors

Fine-tip glue applicator or toothpick

Elmer's clear-drying liquid glue

***Project notes:*** *Refer to project photos and Quilled Shape Gallery when forming quilled shapes. Use a fine-tip glue applicator or toothpick to place glue on ends of quilling paper when securing quilled shapes. Tweezers can be used to place quilled shapes onto card. Finished tree base is 9 x 12¾ inches. Trim mat and frame finished project as desired.*

## Tree Base

**1.** Copy and trace Large Tree Base Pattern on pages 21 and 23 onto mat board using stylus.

**2.** Apply a thin line of glue a few inches long along the stylus outline of the tree. Begin to place 1/8-inch-wide brown quilling paper on edge, directly on the glue line. Hold the paper until dry enough to hold its shape. Use needle tool to scrape away excess glue. Repeat process to outline whole tree. Use tweezers to help fold paper at points of branches. ***Note:*** *It will take time and patience to outline tree.*

**3.** Roll and shape large **Marquise** pieces from 12-inch lengths of several shades of brown 1/8-inch-wide quilling paper. Make enough to fill entire trunk, keeping in mind coils will compress when inserted into trunk.

**4.** Pour puddle of glue onto scrap paper. Dip quilled pieces lightly into glue using tweezers;

dab off any excess and place into tree trunk, beginning at outermost point of branches. Continue adding pieces close together in random color pattern from branches to base of trunk. At base of trunk, reshape pieces to create flat bottom, if desired.

## Spring

*Note: Refer to the Spring Tree on page 12 to create additional quilled and punched flowers and leaves to fill the Four Seasons Tree Sampler.*

### Teardrop Flower

**1.** Roll and shape five holiday green **Teardrops** from 6-inch-long, ⅛-inch-wide quilling paper strips.

**2.** Form one white **Loose Coil** from 4-inch-long, ⅜-inch-wide quilling paper.

**3.** Assemble flower by gluing rounded end of teardrop petals around loose coil center.

### Punched Butterfly

**1.** Punch Medium Monarch Butterfly from light green and white cardstock. Adhere light green butterfly to scrap of moss green cardstock. Discard white punched butterfly but keep inner pieces that were punched from it.

**2.** Adhere 10 tiny round inner dots from white butterfly and four largest remaining white shapes to corresponding spaces on light green butterfly.

**3.** Carefully cut around light green butterfly on moss green mat. Cut

3-inch strip of moss green ⅛-inch-wide quilling paper lengthwise (making it ¹⁄₁₆ inch). Discard one narrow half strip. Fold other narrow strip into V-shape and roll ends in the same direction to create antennae. Glue antennae to back of butterfly's head.

**4.** Punch another butterfly from moss green cardstock and cut off wings. Glue body onto light green butterfly. Slightly fold butterfly at body so when adhered to mat board, wings will not touch background. Adhere only body section to mat board.

## Summer

*Note: Refer to the Summer Tree on page 14 to create additional quilled and punched flowers and leaves to fill the Four Seasons Tree Sampler.*

### Daisies

**1.** Punch 1-inch Stacking Daisies from light blue and blue text-weight paper. Adhere punched flowers together so petals alternate in color.

**2.** Form a **Loose Coil** from a 4-inch strip of ⅛-inch-wide cadet blue quilling paper; adhere to flower center.

**3.** Repeat steps 1 and 2 to make pink-and-light-pink flower with pink centers.

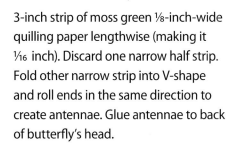

## Wisteria Vines

**1.** Punch 8–10 leaves with 3-Lobe Leaf punch from lavender text-weight paper.

**2.** Roll and shape **Marquise** shapes from 4-inch-long, ⅛-inch-wide lavender, purple and violet quilling paper strips to cover the leaf shapes on the punches. Vary the pattern of purples in the leaves.

**3.** Glue quilling-covered leaf shapes end to end in vinelike pattern. Create three wisteria vines.

## Fringed Flower Buds

**1.** Roll and shape a 3-inch strip of ⅛-inch-wide holiday green quilling paper into a **Grape Roll**. Roll a 3-inch strip of fringed ⅝-inch-wide deep rose paper; adhere to wide end of grape roll piece.

**2.** Roll and shape a 2-inch strip of ⅛-inch-wide pink quilling paper into a **Grape Roll**. Spread apart the fringed flower and adhere the pink grape roll piece into the fringed flower, point side down.

**3.** Make two more flower buds: a lavender fringed flower with a violet center, and a bright yellow fringed flower with a yellow center.

## Husked Flower

**1.** Use a strip of ⅛-inch-wide cadet blue quilling paper and the Flower Husking Diagram on page 22; follow steps 1 and 2 of Husking Basics on page 5.

**2.** Remove the husking; wrap it so the shape (petal) is long and narrow.

**3.** Repeat steps 1 and 2 to create eight cadet blue petals.

**4.** For the flower center, fringe a 2-inch length of ⅜-inch-wide bright yellow quilling paper; adhere a 5-inch strip of ⅛-inch-wide orange quilling paper to the end. Begin rolling a Tight Coil from the orange end of the paper. Fan out fringed portion when finished. Adhere eight petals around this center.

## Husked Sunflower

**1.** Use a strip of ⅛-inch-wide yellow quilling paper and the Sunflower Husking Diagram on page 22; follow steps 1 and 2 of Husking Basics on page 5. Create 80 husked petals to make two sunflowers.

**2.** Finely fringe a strip of ⅜-inch-wide brown quilling paper; adhere it to a full strip of finely fringed ⅝-inch-wide brown quilling paper. Roll the strip, beginning at the end of the ⅜-inch-wide strip.

**3.** Group husked petals into eight groups of five; adhere to fringed center.

## Husked Butterfly

**1.** *Note:* *The husking pattern for the upper butterfly wings is an asymmetrical shape but should be followed like any other pattern.*

Use a strip of 1/16-inch-wide red quilling paper and the Butterfly Husking Diagram on page 22; follow steps 1–3 of Husking Basics on page 5 to make the two upper wings. Use red paper for the first wrapping, remove the shape from the pins and wrap it three more times with 1/16-inch-wide pink paper.

**2.** Create a **Marquise** from a 7-inch-long strip of 1/16-inch-wide orange quilling paper and wrap it in 1/16-inch-wide pink quilling paper three times. Carefully insert this piece into the center loop (pin 2) of the upper wing. Adhere in place.

**3.** Make three **Tight Coils** from 2-inch-long strips of 1/16-inch-wide pink quilling paper and insert into the loop made at pin 5; adhere in place.

**4.** For the bottom wings, follow step 1, starting with pink paper and wrapping with red.

**5.** Roll and shape a **Teardrop** from a 9-inch-long strip of 1/16-inch-wide red quilling paper and insert into center loop (pin 2) of wing. Layer wings on top of each other as shown in photo.

**6.** To create the body, make a **Marquise** from a 10-inch-long strip of 1/8-inch-wide brown quilling paper.

**7.** Cut a short length of 1/8-inch-wide brown quilling paper lengthwise but not quite to the end. Roll ends to create antennae; adhere to tip of body. Adhere wings together and to body as pictured.

### Rainbow Ring Coil

**1.** To create **Ring Coil**, roll a 3/8-inch-wide magenta quilling strip around a 1½-inch-diameter cylinder (such as an empty roll of clear tape), employing the Tuck & Roll Joining Technique on page 5 until the magenta stripe is about 1/16 inch thick. Adhere the end down.

**2.** Adhere a white strip flush to end of magenta strip and repeat step 1. Continue pattern to create turquoise, bright yellow, orange and melon stripes.

### Additional Leaves & Foliage

**1.** To make a variety of large leaves, follow step 4 of Autumn Tree on page 19, using light and medium green quilling paper strips.

**2.** To make other smaller leaves, create **Marquise** or **Shaped Marquise** pieces from 6-inch or 8-inch strips of various green quilling paper strips. Make a few **Modified V Scrolls** to fill in spaces.

## Autumn

*Note: Refer to the Autumn Tree on page 17 to create additional quilled and punched flowers and leaves to fill the Four Seasons Tree Sampler.*

### Marquise Flower

**1.** Roll 10 **Marquise** shapes from 8-inch lengths of 1/8-inch-wide red quilling paper to make two five-petal flowers.

**2.** Roll three Tight Coils per flower from 2-inch lengths of 1/8-inch-

wide deep red quilling paper. Refer to photo to assemble flowers.

### Husked Tulip Leaf

**1.** Use a strip of 1/8-inch-wide bright yellow quilling paper and the Tulip Leaf Husking Diagram on page 22; follow steps 1–3 of Husking Basics on page 5 to make two Tulip Leaf shapes. Be careful wrapping the perimeter of this concave shape by gently forcing a curve between dots 3 and 5, 5 and 7 and slightly between 7 and 9. Add additional pins if necessary to keep the shape. Flip one of the shapes over, match up symmetrically and adhere together along line between dots 1 and 10.

**2.** Cut a 5-inch length of 1/8-inch-wide bright yellow quilling paper; fold in half and adhere to base of leaf as a stem.

### Husked Oak Leaf

**1.** Use a strip of 1/8-inch-wide brown quilling paper and the Oak Leaf Husking Diagram on page 22; follow steps 1–3 of Husking Basics on page 5 to make the three pieces of the Husked

Oak Leaf. Add extra pins to rounded sections to keep the shape, if needed.

**2.** Adhere top piece between dots 8 and 9 to middle piece between dots 3 and 4. Adhere bottom piece between dots 3 and 4 to middle piece between dots 7 and 8.

**3.** Cut a length of brown quilling paper approximately 5 inches long; fold in half and adhere to leaf base as a stem.

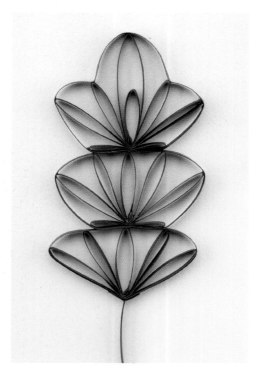

### Husked Maple Leaf

**1.** Use a strip of ⅛-inch-wide orange quilling paper and the Maple Leaf Husking Diagram on page 22; follow steps 1–3 of Husking Basics on page 5 to make one large and two small Husked Maple Leaf shapes. ***Note: Even though these shapes are more angular than the other leaves, you may still need to add additional pins to hold the shape.***

**2.** When dry, remove Husked Maple Leaf shape from pins; flip one of the smaller shapes. Adhere smaller shapes to left and right of large shape, lining up dots 10 on left and right shapes to dots 13 and 14 on center shape.

**3.** Cut a 5-inch length of ⅛-inch-wide orange quilling paper; fold in half and adhere to leaf base as a stem.

### Heart-Shaped Leaf

**1.** Roll and shape two 12-inch lengths of ⅛-inch-wide deep red quilling paper into **Teardrops**. Adhere shapes together, starting at points, to make heart shape.

**2.** Cut a 5-inch length of ⅛-inch-wide deep red quilling paper; fold in half and adhere to leaf as a stem.

## Winter

*Note: Refer to the Winter Tree on page 19 to create additional quilled and punched snowflakes to fill the Four Seasons Tree Sampler.*

### Icicles

**1.** Create spiral by wrapping ⅛-inch-wide silver/gray quilling paper around needle tool.

**2.** Cut finished spiral to about 1 inch. Create five or six icicles and adhere to tree.

### Snowflakes

Use 1⁄16-inch-wide quilling paper cut to 1-inch lengths to create shapes to make two of each snowflake, one blue and one white:

**Snowflake A:** 6 Marquise, 6 Heart Scroll, 6 Y Scroll, 6 Loose Coil.

**Snowflake B:** 6 Marquise, 6 Loose Coil, 6 Y Scroll, 6 Heart Scroll.

**Snowflake C:** 12 Loose Coil, 6 Y Scroll, 6 Marquise.

**Snowflake E:** 12 Marquise, 6 C Scroll, 6 Y Scroll.

**Snowflake D:** 6 Tight Coil, 6 Marquise, 6 Y Scroll, 6 Heart Scroll.

### Final Assembly

**1.** After trunk and seasons quilled shapes are completed, lay out shapes onto tree to see how they fit together. Allow seasons to flow into one another. You may need to make more flowers, leaves, etc., to fill the space, or you might not have to use all you've already made. Consider placing some leaves and snowflakes as if falling from tree.

**2.** Cut sticky portion of a few sticky notes into curves or strips and use as guidelines to keep quadrants of tree seasons in balance. Remove a few quilled shapes at a time, apply glue and adhere them to the tree. Remove or rearrange sticky notes as you work. ■

# Spring Tree

Never yet was a springtime, when the buds forgot to bloom.
—Margaret Elizabeth Sangster

## Materials

Cardstock: light yellow, brown, white, bright green, lime green, various greens

Quilling paper strips: Lake City Craft (⅛-inch-wide white, pale green, leaf green, soft green; ¹⁄₁₆-inch-wide pale green); Paplin Products (⅛-inch-wide lime; ¹⁄₁₆-inch-wide lime)

Punches: EK Success (Mini Flower, Martha Stewart Rose Leaf, Frond); Punch Bunch (Mini Flower 2)

Embossing stylus

Quilling tool

Self-closing tweezers

Paper crimper

Fine-tip glue applicator or toothpick

Elmer's clear-drying liquid glue

Adhesive foam tape

**Project notes:** *Refer to project photos and Quilled Shape Gallery when forming quilled shapes. Use a fine-tip glue applicator or toothpick to place glue on ends of quilling paper when securing quilled shapes. Tweezers can be used to place quilled shapes onto card.*

**1.** Form a 5½ x 8½-inch card from light yellow cardstock.

**2.** Copy and trace Small Tree Base Pattern from page 22 onto brown cardstock; cut out and adhere to card front.

**3.** Copy Scalloped Sentiment Panel from page 21 onto bright green cardstock; cut out and attach to card front with foam tape.

**4.** For small six-petal flower, roll and shape a 4-inch length of white quilling paper into a **Tear Drop**. Repeat five more times for a total of six petals. For center, roll an 11½-inch length of ¹⁄₁₆-inch-wide lime quilling paper into a  **Tight Coil**. Referring to photo, adhere petals and center together to create flower. In the same manner, create the following small six-petal flowers: two additional white and three green with pale green centers. There should be a total of six small six-petal flowers.

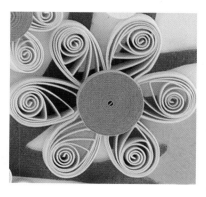 **5.** For large six-petal flower, roll and shape a 6-inch length of soft green quilling paper into a **Teardrop**. Repeat five more times for a total of six petals. For center, roll an 18-inch length of ¹⁄₁₆-inch-wide pale green quilling paper into a **Tight Coil**. Referring to photo, adhere petals and center together to create flower. In the same manner, create the following large six-petal flowers: two additional green and three white with lime centers. There should be a total of six large six-petal flowers.

**6.** For two-layer, six-petal flower, roll and shape an 8-inch length of ⅛-inch-wide pale green quilling paper into a **Teardrop**. Repeat five more times for a total of six large

petals. Repeat six times using a 6-inch length of ⅛-inch-wide pale green quilling paper for a total of six small petals. For center, roll a 6-inch length of leaf green quilling  paper into a **Loose Coil**; band with an 8-inch length of crimped white quilling paper. Referring to photo, adhere petals and center together to create flower.

 **7.** For large six-petal flower with decorative loops, roll and shape a 7-inch length of ⅛-inch-wide lime quilling paper into a **Teardrop**. Repeat five more times for a total of six petals. For decorative loops, shape a 1-inch length of soft green quilling paper into a loop. Repeat five more times for a total of six loops. For center, roll a 6-inch length of pale green quilling paper into a **Loose Coil**. Referring to photo, adhere petals, loops and center together to create flower.

**8.** For small green and white punched flowers, punch one white Mini Flower and one lime Mini Flower 2 shape. Snip between white petals stopping short of center; layer and adhere flowers together, shaping petals as shown. Repeat five more  times for a total of six layered flowers.

**9.** Punch five rose leaves and six frond shapes from desired cardstock; add veins with stylus.

**10.** Referring to photo, adhere quilled flowers and leaves to card front. ∎

# Summer Tree

There shall be
eternal summer
in the grateful heart.
~Celia Thaxter

## Materials

Cardstock: light pink, medium pink, magenta, white, black, red, tan, brown, yellow, orange

Text-weight paper: yellow, bright yellow, white

Quilling paper strips: Lake City Craft (⅛-inch-wide deep red, red, pink, lavender, violet, purple, tan, light blue, deep blue, periwinkle, deep green, turquoise, bright yellow, black); Paplin Products (⅝-inch-wide magenta, ¾-inch-wide red)

Quilling tools: slotted, needle

Quilled Creations Fringed Mums die set

Die-cutting machine

Punches: Fiskars (6-Petal Punch); Punch Bunch (Mini Flower 2, Stamen small, Blossom small); EK Success (Paper Shapers 5-Petal Flower, Martha Stewart 3-in-1 Hydrangea medium); ⅛-inch circle

Embossing stylus: 2mm, 6mm

Quilled Creations Circle Template Board

Self-closing tweezers

Fine-tip glue applicator or toothpick

Foam pad

Elmer's clear-drying liquid glue

Paper adhesive

Adhesive foam tape

*Project notes: Refer to project photos and Quilled Shape Gallery when forming quilled shapes. Use a fine-tip glue applicator or toothpick to place glue on ends of quilling paper when securing quilled shapes. Tweezers can be used to place quilled shapes onto card.*

**1.** Form a 5½ x 8½-inch card from medium pink cardstock.

**2.** Copy and trace Small Tree Base Pattern from page 22 onto brown cardstock; cut out and adhere to card front.

**3.** Copy Scalloped Sentiment Panel from page 21 onto light pink cardstock; cut out and attach to card front with foam tape.

**4.** For Malaysian flower, begin by rolling an 11-inch length of periwinkle quilling paper into a circle using an ¹¹⁄₁₆-inch-diameter circle template. Use tweezers to remove coil and glue end closed. Gently squeeze circle to make a long, narrow  oval shape. Pinch ends of oval around tweezers creating a **Malaysian Teardrop**. *Note: A Malaysian Teardrop is made as for a Crescent, and then the points are joined and glued together.* Apply glue to points of teardrop and secure points together with self-closing tweezers to dry. Repeat six more times for a total of seven petals. For center, roll and shape a 12-inch length of deep blue quilling paper into a **Grape Roll**. Referring to photo,  adhere petals and center together to create flower. In the same manner, create one additional Malaysian flower with light blue petals.

**5.** For medium fringed mum, begin by using medium fringed mum die to cut two lengths from yellow text-weight paper. Cut one length in half. Glue one half of fringed length to end of full fringed length end to end. Follow the steps to make a **Basic**

**Fringed Flower** on page 4 to complete the flower. In the same manner, create three additional medium fringed mums.

**6.** For gerbera daisy, begin by using large fringed mum die to cut two lengths from white text-weight paper. Use small fringed mum die to cut one length from bright yellow text-weight paper. Glue two white lengths together end to end followed by bright yellow length to create one long strip. Glue a 12-inch length of bright yellow quilling paper to end of bright yellow fringed length. Beginning with bright yellow end, use slotted tool to roll entire strip keeping coil even at end. Glue coil closed. Remove roll by gently pushing it off tool. Open flower by holding it in both hands and gently fluffing fringe with thumbs. *Note: If needed, insert back end of quilling tool into flower center to smooth out any unevenness.*

**7.** For posy, begin by rolling a 2-inch length of deep red quilling paper into a **Loose Coil** formed in a ³⁄₁₆-inch circle template. Repeat five more times for  a total of six petals. For center, roll a 2-inch length of tan quilling paper into a **Loose Coil**. Referring to photo, adhere petals and center together to create flower. In the same manner, create two additional posies.

**8.** For forget-me-not, roll and shape a 2-inch length of turquoise quilling paper into a **Marquise**. Repeat four more times for a total of five petals. For center, cut a 2-inch length of bright yellow quilling paper in half lengthwise creating a ¹⁄₁₆-inch-wide strip; roll strip into a **Tight Coil**. Referring to photo, adhere petals and center together to create flower. In the same manner, create one additional forget-me-not.

**9.** For multihued violets, roll and shape a 6-inch length of lavender quilling paper into a **Teardrop** formed in a ¹¹⁄₃₂-inch-diameter circle template. Repeat four more times for a total of five petals using violet and purple quilling paper as desired. For center, use ⅛-inch hole punch to punch a circle from yellow cardstock. Referring to photo, adhere petals and center together to create flower. In the same manner, create two additional violets.

**10.** For punched blossom, begin by rolling a 3-inch length of ⅛-inch-wide red quilling paper into a **Tight Coil**. Use Blossom small punch to punch a flower from red cardstock. Punch a circle

from tan cardstock. Glue tan circle to center of red flower; glue tight coil to back of flower. In the same manner, create one additional punched blossom flower.

**11.** For punched hydrangea, begin by rolling a 3-inch length of pink quilling paper into a **Tight Coil**. Use 3-in-1 Hydrangea medium to punch a flower from light pink cardstock; only the largest of the three pieces will be used to create the hydrangea. Discard the other two pieces. Punch three ⅛-inch circles from white cardstock. Glue three circles to center of flower; glue Tight Coil to back of flower. In the same manner, create one additional punched hydrangea flower.

**12.** For modified primrose, use Stamen small punch to punch a stamen from orange cardstock. Use 5-Petal Flower punch to punch a flower from yellow cardstock; use 6-Petal Punch to punch a flower from magenta cardstock. Carefully snip between petals on magenta and yellow flowers stopping before center. Place flowers and stamen on foam pad and use 6mm embossing stylus to rub centers in a circular motion to shape outer edges. Layer and adhere flowers and stamen together. In the same manner, create one additional modified primrose flower.

**13.** For mini anemone, use Mini Flower 2 punch to punch two flowers from black cardstock. Use 5-Petal Flower punch to punch two flowers from white cardstock. In the same manner as in step 12, snip petals and shape flowers

using 2mm embossing stylus for black flowers. Layer and adhere flowers together offsetting petals as shown. In the same manner, create two additional mini anemone flowers.

**14.** For folded rose, begin by slipping the end of an 8-inch length of magenta quilling paper into slotted tool from the left. Follow the steps to make a **Folded Rose** on page 4 to complete the flower. Repeat to make a second rose using a 16-inch length of ¾-inch-wide red quilling paper.

**15.** For leaves, roll and shape a 4-inch length of deep green quilling paper into a **Marquise**. Repeat as desired to create nine or more leaves.

**16.** Referring to photo, arrange and adhere flowers and leaves to card front. ∎

# Autumn Tree

Autumn is a second spring when every leaf is a flower.

~Albert Camus

## Materials

Cardstock: burnt orange, orange, brown, yellow, crimson, burgundy, gold

⅛-inch-wide quilling paper strips: deep red, crimson, orange, bright yellow, brown, tan, taupe, mustard, pumpkin

Slotted quilling tool

Punches: Punch Bunch (Maple Leaf 2 Medium, Oak Leaf Medium); EK Success (Martha Stewart Rose Leaf)

2mm embossing stylus

Self-closing tweezers

Fine-tip glue applicator or toothpick

Foam pad

Elmer's clear-drying liquid glue

Paper adhesive

Adhesive foam tape

*Project notes: Refer to project photos and Quilled Shape Gallery when forming quilled shapes. Use a fine-tip glue applicator or toothpick to place glue on ends of quilling paper when securing quilled shapes. Tweezers can be used to place quilled shapes onto card.*

**1.** Form a 5½ x 8½-inch card from burnt orange cardstock.

**2.** Copy and trace Small Tree Base Pattern from page 22 onto brown cardstock; cut out and adhere to card front.

**3.** Copy Scalloped Sentiment Panel from page 21 onto gold cardstock; cut out and attach to card front with foam tape as shown.

**4.** For large leaf, roll and shape a 6-inch length of desired inner color quilling paper into a **Marquise**. Repeat four more times for a total of five pieces. Wrap each piece four times using desired outer color quilling paper. Glue the shaped marquises together at their points to loosely resemble the finished leaf; wrap shape four times with the outer color quilling paper. In the same manner, create two additional large leaves using different colors of quilling paper.

**5.** For multicolored frond leaf, roll and shape a 4-inch length of desired quilling paper into a **Teardrop**. Repeat six more times for a total of seven pieces. Using a 1- to 2-inch scrap of brown quilling paper for stem, glue stem to point of one teardrop, and then glue the six remaining teardrops in pairs with points meeting on each side of the stem. In the same manner, create three additional multicolored frond leaves.

**6.** For small leaf, roll and shape a 4-inch length of desired color quilling paper into a **Teardrop**, **Marquise** or **Shaped Marquise**. Repeat four more times for a total of five pieces. Arrange like colors into twos and threes to create leaf shapes. Glue shapes together at their points and glue to a scrap of like-colored paper as a stem. In the same manner, create a total of 11 small leaves.

**7.** Punch leaf shapes in a variety of colors as desired; add veins using stylus.

**8.** Referring to photo, arrange and adhere leaves to card front. ■

# Winter Tree

Snow falling soundlessly
in the middle of the night
will always fill my heart
with sweet clarity.
~Novala Takemoto

## Materials

Cardstock: white, blue, brown

Text-weight paper: white, blue

¹⁄₁₆-inch-wide quilling paper strips: white, blue

Slotted quilling tool

Punches: Punch Bunch (Small Snowflake); Hobby Lobby/The Paper Studio (1-inch Snowflake)

Circle template

Self-closing tweezers

Fine-tip glue applicator or toothpick

Elmer's clear-drying liquid glue

Adhesive foam tape

*Project notes: Refer to project photos and Quilled Shape Gallery when forming quilled shapes. Use a fine-tip glue applicator or toothpick to place glue on ends of quilling paper when securing quilled shapes. Tweezers can be used to place quilled shapes onto card.*

**1.** Form a 5½ x 8½-inch card from blue cardstock.

**2.** Copy and trace Small Tree Base Pattern from page 22 onto brown cardstock; cut out and adhere to card front.

**3.** Copy Scalloped Sentiment Panel from page 21 onto white cardstock; cut out and attach to card front with foam tape.

**4.** For Snowflake A, roll and shape a 1½-inch length of white quilling paper into a **Teardrop** formed in a ⁹⁄₆₄-inch circle template. Repeat five times for a total of six pieces. Roll and shape a 2-inch length of white quilling paper into a **Teardrop** formed in an ¹¹⁄₆₄-inch circle template. Repeat five times for a total of six pieces. Roll and shape a 2-inch length of white quilling paper into a **Y Scroll**. Repeat five times for a total of six pieces. Adhere pieces together as shown to form a snowflake. In the same manner, create a second snowflake using blue quilling paper.

**5.** For Snowflake B, roll and shape a 1½-inch length of white quilling paper into a **Marquise** formed in a ⁹⁄₆₄-inch circle template. Repeat five times for a total of six pieces. Roll and shape a 2-inch length of white quilling paper into a **Y Scroll**. Repeat five times for a total of six pieces. Roll and shape a 1½-inch length of white quilling paper into a **Heart Scroll**. Repeat five times for a total of six pieces. Adhere pieces together as shown

to form snowflake. In the same manner, create a second snowflake using blue quilling paper.

**6.** For Snowflake C, roll and shape a 1-inch length of white quilling paper into a **Loose Coil**. Repeat six times for a total of seven pieces. Roll and shape a 2-inch length of white quilling paper into a **Y Scroll**. Repeat five times for a total of six pieces. Roll and shape a 2-inch length of white quilling paper into a **Marquise** formed in an ¹¹⁄₆₄-inch circle template. Repeat five times for a total of six pieces. Adhere pieces together as shown to form snowflake. In the same manner, create a second snowflake using blue quilling paper.

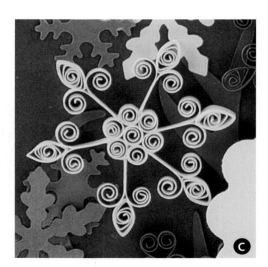

**7.** Punch various-size snowflakes from text-weight paper.

**8.** Referring to photo, arrange and adhere quilled and punched snowflakes to card front. ■

Match on line to make complete pattern

A

**Four Seasons Tree Sampler**
Large Tree Base Pattern

B          D

Autumn is a second spring when every leaf is a flower.
~Albert Camus

**Scalloped Sentiment Panel**
Autumn

*Never yet was a springtime, when the buds forgot to bloom.*
*~Margaret Elizabeth Sangster*

**Scalloped Sentiment Panel**
Spring

Snow falling soundlessly in the middle of the night will always fill my heart with sweet clarity.
~Novala Takemoto

**Scalloped Sentiment Panel**
Winter

There shall be eternal summer in the grateful heart.
~Celia Thaxter

**Scalloped Sentiment Panel**
Summer

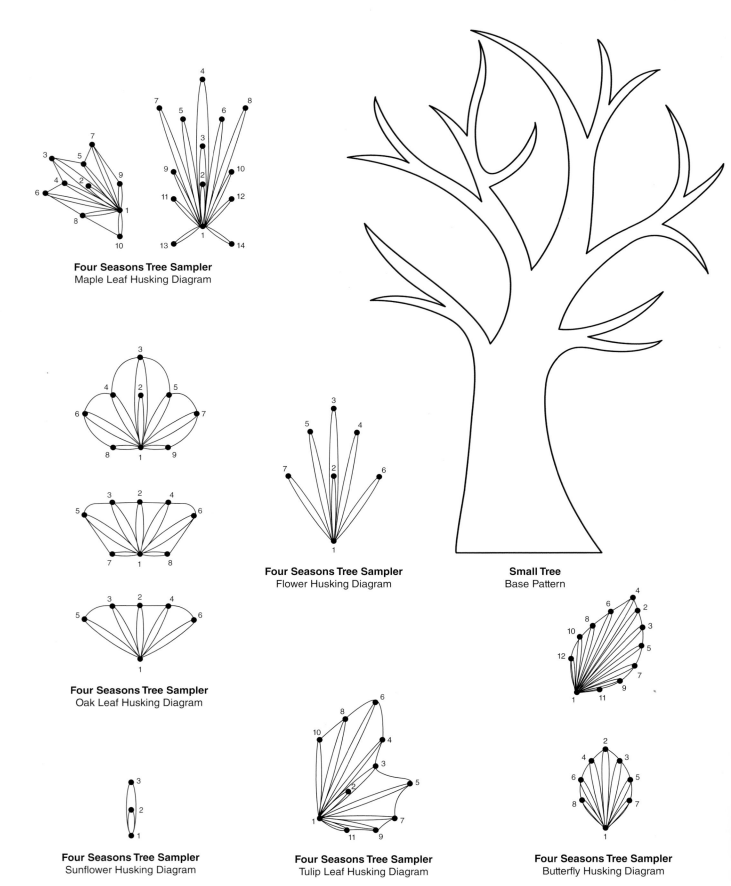

**Four Seasons Tree Sampler**
Maple Leaf Husking Diagram

**Four Seasons Tree Sampler**
Oak Leaf Husking Diagram

**Four Seasons Tree Sampler**
Sunflower Husking Diagram

**Four Seasons Tree Sampler**
Flower Husking Diagram

**Small Tree**
Base Pattern

**Four Seasons Tree Sampler**
Tulip Leaf Husking Diagram

**Four Seasons Tree Sampler**
Butterfly Husking Diagram

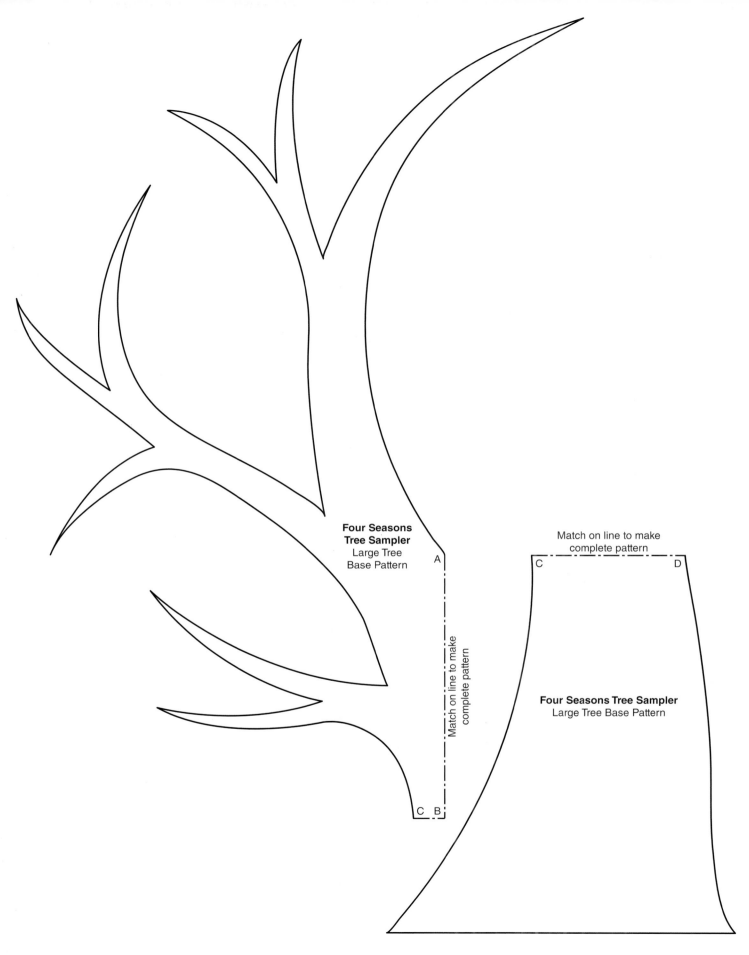

**Four Seasons Tree Sampler**
Large Tree Base Pattern

A

B

C

Match on line to make complete pattern

Match on line to make complete pattern

C                                    D

**Four Seasons Tree Sampler**
Large Tree Base Pattern

# Buyer's Guide

**EK Success**
www.eksuccessbrands.com

**Elmer's® Products Inc.**
(888) 435-6377
www.elmers.com

**Fiskars**
(866) 348-5661
www2.fiskars.com

**Hobby Lobby Stores Inc.**
www.hobbylobby.com

**Lake City Craft**
(417) 725-8444
www.quilling.com

**McGill Inc.**
(904) 482-0091
www.mcgillinc.com

**Paplin Products**
(440) 572-1086
www.paplin.com

**Punch Bunch Inc.**
(719) 686-5300
www.thepunchbunch.com

**Quilled Creations Inc.**
(877) 784-5533
www.quilledcreations.com

*The Buyer's Guide listings are provided as a service to our readers and should not be considered an endorsement from this publication.*

# About the Author

Shelly Krzyzewski has been quilling since 2007 and is an active member of the North American Quilling Guild (www.naqg.org). She enjoys many types of paper art, from quilling to making paper beads to creating life-size paper flower bouquets. Shelly and her husband live in South Bend, Ind., where she has been an elementary school teacher for 11 years.

**Annie's®** *Four Seasons of Quilling* is published by Annie's, 306 East Parr Road, Berne, IN 46711. Printed in USA. Copyright © 2015 Annie's. All rights reserved. This publication may not be reproduced in part or in whole without written permission from the publisher.

**RETAIL STORES:** If you would like to carry this publication or any other Annie's publication, visit AnniesWSL.com.

Every effort has been made to ensure that the instructions in this publication are complete and accurate. We cannot, however, take responsibility for human error, typographical mistakes or variations in individual work. Please visit AnniesCustomerService.com to check for pattern updates.

ISBN: 978-1-57367-658-8

1 2 3 4 5 6 7 8 9